I0224647

Sleep Bringer

poems by

Daniel Ruefman

Finishing Line Press
Georgetown, Kentucky

Sleep Bringer

For all sleep bringers, mine and yours

ACKNOWLEDGMENTS

I would like to thank the editors of the following publications, in which the
following poems have previously appeared, often in earlier forms:

Adelaide Magazine – "Arthur," "Tears of Johannesburg," & "Deserted City"
Barely South Review – "What are you having?"
FLARE: The Flagler Review – "Remit and Renewal," "Beyond the
Butterscotch," & "A telling reconciliation"
Foliate Oak Literary Magazine – "The Carpet"
Junto Magazine – "Canoeing Canaveral"
Minetta Review – "Principled Dissent"
Mothers Always Write – "Learning Under High Bridge," "Sleep Bringer," &
"There You Were"
Red Cedar Review – "Mind the Trolls," "Black Swing," & "Socrates Had It
Right"
Sediments Literary-Arts Review – "Never Seen"
SLAB: Sound and Literary Arts Book – "Virginia Napalm"
Tonopah Review – "Pulse"
Wisconsin's Poets Calendar – "Commute" & "Standoff on a Hair Trigger"

Special thanks to Andy Cochran and Kevin Drzakowski who served as
critical readers for these works during their development. Your insights
made all the difference.

Publisher: Leah Maines
Editor: Christen Kincaid
Cover Art: Brandy N. Donze
Author Photo: Daniel Ruefman
Cover Design: Leah Huete

Printed in the USA on acid-free paper.
Order online: www.finishinglinepress.com
        also available on amazon.com

Author inquiries and mail orders:
Finishing Line Press
P. O. Box 1626
Georgetown, Kentucky 40324
U. S. A.

Table of Contents

III

I.

Spontaneity

The Monday before Spring Break,
my office phone rang and her goading voice
on the other end was all
crazy talk—

so we cancelled the priest
who had counseled us since summer
and drove through spring snowdrifts
to meet the minister willing to work Black Saturday;

we abandoned the Episcopal chapel in Westfield
and booked Hurlbut Methodist at Chautauqua,
moved our August cake to March,
and in our haste, misprinted the invitations to no one;

we applied for our marriage license with a clerk
who studied our intended surname, murmuring *I can't do that,*
then noticing that the business hours were dying,
declared, *if Albany doesn't like it, they'll send it back.*

A week later, she strode down the aisle,
her father lifting a fistful of her unhemmed gown,
and I stood to greet her in that one spot of sunlight
that squinted between plywood boards on the broken window.

When she took my hand, I drifted for a while
in the blue-gray ocean of her iris,
and listened to the piano woman play
the end of the "Feather Theme;"

her friends chortled into the camcorder,
panning between guests and bridal party
as her brother and sister read from a book at the pulpit,
until there was some mention of the rings;

and the minister was all—*do you?*
and we were all—*yes.*

What are you having?

My first thought was a Velociraptor,
so my progeny would have the speed and visage
to dominate whatever track, or field, or pitch,

      but judging from the curve of my wife's pubic bone

she may as well have a dolphin,
with mind enough to reason, or socialize,
or swimming abilities that evade me still,

      but considering the elasticity of her birth canal,

she may have something more like a gibbon, or baboon,
or orangutan, something with opposable thumbs,
dexterous digits, to grab, or hold, or carry.

Or was your real question
Do you know the sex of your baby?
Ask my wife if she knows;

      find out how much she cares.

Sleep Bringer

In the dark, my son slaps
at my three-day-old scruff
and I recall the texture
of my father's face when camping,
when his electric razor would die
allowing a salt-and-pepper shadow
to crawl back across his chin;

I remember kneading his face
between the heels of my hands
to identify the person
lifting me out of the steel sink
in a Cook Forest bathhouse;

or perhaps I can imagine
how it must have been
to be small and loved
that I imagine myself
in my son's place, stroking
the coarse grain of a cheek,
tracing its edges

in a darkened room, shade pulled
to block out the starlight reflecting
from the season's first snow,
swaying steady in the arms
of an awkward giant—
the sleep bringer
shushing the darkness.

Learning Under High Bridge

My son dangles his limbs
Through the rungs in the rail
under High Bridge, where the Mississippi
cuts its channel through St. Paul;
in a language all his own,
he chirps and points as if to say,
This—this means log. See it floating?
That—that is a riverboat. Daddy, say it with me?

He points, in turn, to the concrete footings,
steel scaffolding of the bridge, at a plastic bag
caught in the current, bound for Lower Town,
and with each abstract burble, pop, and squeal,
he names things he will translate for me
later, and I try not to see the inky blackness
sweeping one meter below his toes,
and I tell myself that his body cannot fit
in the space between the steel bars,

and yet my mind flickers to an image of him
in the current, and me giving chase,
my useless limbs flailing, unable to
pull my mass through the water,
unable to grasp a leg or arm
as he is swallowed by the covetous stream,
like everything that bloats this river while it
consumes the whole of every tributary
from Minnesota to the Gulf of Mexico;

but I force out the image and remind myself
that he is safe here—he cannot fall into
the river he names *dur-da*;
he reaches for a stick floating out of reach
past the footings toward the city;
he waves to the people on the boat,
to the couple jogging along the far bank,
toward the city he may one day call *home*.

Lookout Ridge

A ten-year old's heel connects
and my right contact falls
folded on the plastic stairs
of the indoor playground;

with a child in my lap, I slip
through the staggered crevices,
past the green slide, and
down the faux rock face;

to the right, a twelve-year-old flails
in the blue bounce house,
threading belly flops through bodies
of toddling two-year olds

while his mother streams **TLC**
on her iPad in the corner,
sound dampening headphones in place
and when her son emerges

complaining of thirst, she reaches blindly
for her bag, places a change purse in his hand
and points to the drink cooler
by the front desk;

I watch when he returns with a 16 oz.
throwback can of *Surge*
and with a hiss and crack *Lookout*
is transformed from noun to verb
as children fall like missiles
screaming toward ground zero

and I hear the wail of the cone-shaped sirens
perched on those false bluffs,
as we duck and cover
waiting for the unexploded ordinance
to pop.

Inbox Anger

Your anger inundates my inbox
in response to the out-of-office message

> *We deserve more.*
> *We aren't nobodies here.*

Yet you don't care
that our son is losing weight so fast
that the doctor is threatening hospitalization,
so that every two hours, we attack
syringe in hand, waterboarding him
with cocktails of breastmilk and formula;

> *We deserve this joy*
> *in pictures.*

Yet you don't care
that I am plugging our son into the wall
with an extension cord, just long enough
to reach the kitchen, or that the neighbors
interrogate me each time I step outside
to discuss the medical supply truck
that came to offload twice in two days.

> *Remember where you came from.*
> *Without family, you would be nothing.*

But you don't care
that my wife is still bleeding from the birth,
or that our minds are drifting somewhere
in post-partum limbo, both of us torn
between our obligations here.

> *We deserve personal emails.*
> *We deserve pictures.*

Shall I unplug my son, then,
and unwrap the wires
that tether him to the humming box
between bassinet and baseboard?

> *It only takes five minutes*
> *to put on that outfit we sent you.*

After all

> *Five minutes won't hurt him.*

But why would you ask that we risk it?

There You Were
(In Memory of Alistair)

At the first sonogram,
we searched the screen
and there you were,
with your brother,
in Mama's belly.

Your big brother played
with cars on the floor
while Mama and I gazed
up at the screen.
When the doctor said "two,"

our mouths gaped,
our insides swelled, and we imagined
bringing you home,
watching as you and Quinton
settled some score with Titus.

You were small then,
but in that moment, we knew
you had heart enough for the name
Alistair—a friend,
defender of all.

We watched you grow,
we listened to the steady whoosh
of your heart
and when things got tight,
there you were;

When the flat of a palm found
that place where you sat,
you prodded and poked back,
with fingers, foot, or buttocks
and there you were, living in our smiles.

The morning you followed your brother
into that room, we cradled you
in the crooks of our arms, loving you—
needing your presence, and when our tears came,

we closed our eyes,
and there you were.

Black Swing

A black swing sways
behind my heart;
it twinges as it tugs
wearing raw the sinews
that suspend it there.

A black swing sways
vacant
beyond the sightlines
of the pregnant couple next door
or the twins down the street.

A black swing sways
where there is no wind,
no hand to impose its will,
as it slips like the new moon
lower, toward my liver.

A black swing sways,
sighing like the will-o-wisps
displacing space—quiet;
do you hear it too?
Or did you never even know

it was there?

Pulse

Living cocotte,
the rattle of maypoles and junipers;
vigorous pulse of the bawd at the door
shake the nerves of the sub-sentient;

preeclampsia,
delicate shrieks and deep burr
of both Maryologists and pricks;
this house will be silent soon;

consumed
for one evening,
reveling in what lies between
the maypoles and junipers,

the existential screams of time—
the thin and evasive,
the thick and deliberate
spinning the windburn of lamentation

unto a silent mourning.

Broken

I.

I waited for your fingers
to open and accept my own,
the way your brother's had;

your willowy limbs,
deceptively warm,
were bent and swaddled.

When I cradled your head,
your mouth fell open
and for a moment,

it was like you were drawing breath,
your malleable muscles slackening,
as if sighing in a supine slumber.

At 5:00 in the morning,
I peeled back the receiving blanket
thick with meconium,

and wrapped you in the only diaper
you would ever wear.
Carrie—the nurse—helped me

to thread your arms through
the matching blue and white pajamas
we had planned to take you home in;

as she shifted your weight,
the shadows moved
and I waited for a scream.

It never came.

II.

When the coroner came,
your brother suckled
skin-to-skin

as the man emphasized urgency,
to get you on the slab
in the St. Paul mortuary

as if he believed that you were never
a son or brother or nephew,
as if dying in the womb lessened the loss of you.

When he had finished his work,
we saw you swaddled at the funeral home
abated warmth became cold wetness.

The sutures oozed,
saturating the fabric you were wrapped in,
your cold blood sticky against my palm.

III.

For weeks, the cards came
forcing on me sentiments of faith,
riddled with biblical references,

things that I never believed.
Some spoke of prayers
and I wondered how many

had actually bent a knee bedside in the night
and allowed your name
to touch their lips.

Some people spoke of fate—fuck fate
fuck the faux consolation of
at least you have one.

Fuck the man who cut you,
who held your heart in his hands
who weighed your insides

like a butcher behind the deli counter,
leaving us to mourn in the vacuum
created by your absence.

Fuck their gestures,
fuck their sentiment—

I am broken.

Beauty

When he first met her,
beauty was encapsulated by
the riptide in the ocean of her iris,
pulling and ensnaring him
in the tangled curls draped
over her pale shoulder.

When beauty intensified,
he married her
and on their wedding night,
he rubbed oil into her shoulders,
feeling it warm against her skin;
with the tips of his fingers,
he traced the muscles
that ran along the length of her spine,
to the dimples of her lower back;
he felt the shape of her buttocks
against his hands, memorizing
her form in the candlelight.

When their first son was born,
she whispered her greeting
in bloodied bath water,
her child still tethered to her
by the cord that vanished
between the peaks of her knees
and she became more radiant—
more pure.

Years later,
he dreamt still of beauty, maturing,
more savory and sweet and seductive
than the finest red wine
or the sharpest Wisconsin cheddar;
he wanted her to come to him,
wake him for midnight succor,
but instead she sat in the glider
beside an empty crib in the baby's room,
staring blankly into her phone
without reason.

It was in those quiet hours
that he found the clubs,
the live shows of burlesque bodies
each a fraction of what hers was to him,
and yet, he filled himself
with wanton need,
always returning home
to find her in the glider,
more dissatisfied
and twice as empty.

Never Seen

She peeks through the blinds
as her husband dips a hose
in the blue plastic pool,
across the yard from their daughters,
motionless in their red Power Wheels,
towels draped, waiting
for word that the water is ready.

He lights a cigarette,
grips it between his yellow teeth,
grins and waves at the neighbor mowing
an adjacent, square plot of suburbia;
his dog stirs the contents
of the pool with his legs,
lapping it up as he moves.

Inside, she wrangles brown bottles
from his one-man-party,
in the game room, office,
bathroom, and kitchen,
until the sound of bag on bag
chimes in the bin.

While their girls splash in the water,
he unwraps the foil
from a Bartles and Jaymes,
downs it in one, sets the bottle
on the trunk of his car,
and pulls another from the fridge,

in denial of the threat
living in the manila folders
on the kitchen counter
next to the calendar
with weeks ticked off in red,
and only two days until the words
divorce final.

Reflection of a Corpse

Swept from the corner
to the center of the garage, the desiccated
sentinel toad was as flat and dry
as October leaves on the floor.

Last summer, he squatted, bulbous
on the front stoop and my wife whispered
her salutations on her way to work,
while he snacked on mosquitoes and biting flies.

He moved in two years ago, when neighbors
on both sides of our lot cured their yards
and he and his brethren sought asylum
from chemicals that burned their bodies;

like the people who clamored for the Hueys
at the Saigon embassy, the lucky found refuge
in our gardens and bark beds; survivors plumped
on grubs and beetles that infested our natural turf.

Our neighbors laughed
each time I stopped mowing and scooped
this one from my path and placed him
in the shade of the hostas alongside the garage.

When the hard freeze came
he must have sought shelter here
learning the hard lesson of a Wisconsin winter
above ground, unable to burrow through concrete.

Socrates Had it Right

When I first read Socrates' claim
that *sin is ignorance,*

> I recalled the obliviousness
> of my mother the day my son died;
> she asked if we could dog sit
> and if I could book her reservations
> at the campground near Willow River;
> when I declined
> she belittled my bereaved wife;
> she said that I deserved this,
> that I brought it on myself,
> that I was my father's son
> that I was *fucking pathetic.*

Later I read Kierkegaard's rebuttal
that *despair is sin*

> and thought how odd it was
> to mourn this way at 33,
> the catatonic state
> descending so fast that
> I forgot to bathe for a week
> as if the black hole in the nursery
> sucked away every ribbon
> of light the universe hurled
> toward earth and no matter
> the cards
> the prayers
> the frozen meals from friends—

Thinking on these views, I know now
that Socrates had it right;

sin is not despair;
it is the ignorance
of empathy,
of love,
of a selfless impulse;

it is the inability to inflict no harm.

After Alistair

From across the hall came
a phonational resonance.

It began with a low hum swelling,
gathering in the gut,

and it rose, predatory, on the updrafts,
like circling hawks or eagles

or like waxen gliders carrying man
like Icarus, to a terminal altitude.

Accompaniment chorused—
a duet, a quartet, a choir

of grating chords
which frayed the myelin sheaths

that tied the nerves of my ears to my neck
and I blenched,

as I struggled to seek its source.
Then in the workroom, I glimpsed my colleagues;

they boomed through downturned,
half-moon eyes.

When next the sound rose,
I recognized it as something

I might have once called a laugh,
and I wondered just how long

since I had heard my own, and how similar
it might have been to those in the workroom

if I had not lost it—
if it had never stopped coming.

Another Child

When you say you want another,
I sit in the narrow space
between crib and toddler bed
thinking of the things accumulated
over the past three years—
six strollers, four carriers,
fourteen diaper boxes filled with clothes
for every season, in every conceivable
shape and color and size.
I think of naptime,
those hours spent rocking
and wringing my hands,
hoping that both of our sons
would sleep without waking
for an hour, always wishing
for success, but rarely finding it.

I love my boys, but I dream of breaks,
of summers spent not lugging diaper bags
to the zoo; time to spend and speak
without the distractions of babies
screaming or crawling toward the stairs
wanting to climb up on things, prying attention
from my eldest who wants me to play.
Three months out of every year,
I watch them solo, tending them
on my own, envying your work schedule,
time spent with adults
who do not steal your phone to watch
Ryan's Toy Review on YouTube.

When you ask me what I want,
my answer is *time*.
Enough to sleep and write,
to breathe and bathe,
in a space to call my own.
I say I love you
and you beg for more, by twos and threes,
and I say I love you still.
But when I think of starting over,
the stress of swaddling and syringe feeding
I admit that I am tired,
and just haven't love enough
left in me for that.

Living Winter

When the weather breaks, head north
to that place where the snow squalls stay,
and wait there by a wood fire
in the cabin on Lake Superior where hoarfrost
glistens on the trees till May.

When snow geese find you, go further
into the land of permafrost
up where the muskoxen munch
on the woody arctic willows
that cling to the rocky outcrops.

When summer strands you in Nunavut,
harvest the sea while you can—
catch king crab, stock salmon
in the smokehouse, and wait
for the ice to come back to you.

When it does, follow the continental cold south,
past the muskoxen plateaus,
pause at the cabin in Grand Marais
just long enough to warm yourself by the fire
until glassine winter skins stretch over 10,000 lakes.

       Then keep going—
       your kids are waiting.

II.

Principled Dissent

When Mr. Ellis told me in metal shop to *make it square,*
I thought of the pockmarked complexion of Venus
de Milo and of the age of her amputations,
porous, weathered, and uneven;

I considered how the spring freckles on beauty's nose
accompanied a renewed radiance that dulled each winter,
and how those russet flecks compared to Cindy Crawford's
mole, which drew all eyes from a porcelain world;

I reveled in subtlety—the tan lines peeking,
the dimples on beauty's thigh,
a patient patina, forming—molecule by molecule—
only recognized by those who appreciate such suggestion.

When he insisted that I *make it square*
I pushed the bubble of my level slightly left, in protest,
scratched two lines and folded the seam,
skewed just enough to make my box off-center, unbalanced,
transecting the room of right angles.

Bodies

(Atlantic Station, Atlanta, GA)

Intricacies of meat,
more than naked,
flayed, frozen, and posed
like department store manikins;
smoker's lungs,
black with tar,
stiffened by resin;
tangled arteries
veins, and nerves,
long-dead,
hung in the glass case,
treated to outlast
those that still bled,
those that still channeled charges;
yet their brittle tips broke and scattered
littering flecks of former flesh
about the bottom of the case—
a reminder that, fight as we do
we all are but new dust
waiting to drop.

Canoeing Canaveral

It's hard to distinguish the living from the dead
when the sun sinks low
behind the hoary oyster beds.

Brittle bone now sharp is shed
a subtle graveyard in the brackish flow
it's hard to distinguish the living from the dead

through the government cut channels, Atlantic bled
tide inhaling, exhaling—high to low
behind the hoary oyster beds.

The water's whisper tells of the survivor's dread
natural wonders carved away to show that
it's hard to distinguish the living from the dead

Gentle dashing across the razor edge,
where generations have turned from life to stone
behind the hoary oyster beds

As the ancient poets might have said
even shellfish have bones and
it's hard to distinguish the living from the dead
behind the hoary oyster beds.

Arthur

There is little that I remember of my grandfather
but the fishing on Lake Erie.
Even now, I see his silhouette perched
atop an upturned five-gallon bucket
on the concrete pier at Presque Isle,
in the shadow of the small lighthouse there;

For bait, I think he preferred salmon eggs to worms,
as there was always a small jar in his tacklebox,
tiny ruby orbs suspended in brine,
so much like Lilliputian maraschino cherries,
that I once plucked one from the jar,
placed it on my tongue—and I never did that again.

I think he must have worn a lot of hats
with the brim pulled low over his eyes,
perhaps to shade the light as he napped,
or maybe it was just to hide the whisper
of his chemo-thin hair, after he began
the too-late treatments for the Lymphoma
that metastasized, just as his retirement
was coming on;

Dad blames the postwar paint shop,
the toxic fumes he huffed
since his honorable discharge
from the Army Air Corps
where he trained soldiers stateside
to find Nazi targets for the B2 Bombers.

I can see his shape, skeletal thin,
his taut suspenders heaving up slack slacks,
his firm grip on the hilt of his rod
a patient patient, waiting for a fish
to rise.

I try to recall my grandfather's face,
But it eludes me,
so I call up the sepia photograph
of the cocksure corporal hugging to him
a nurse with the eyes of my grandmother;
it is all I have of his face,
and I must be content with that.

Remit and Renewal

We change our skin completely,
every 28 days,
a tight new suit to hold our everythings,
generating and regenerating,
cloning scars, sunspots, and moles.
Without it,
unspeakable things would spill
the ugly secrets of life—
liver, stomach, kidneys, and bowels—
the cleansing parts that collect the dirt
and flush it out;
few will touch our coverings
before they are replaced;
briefly some may explore the crevices,
pluck lint from bellybuttons and toes,
scrub away the daily salt,
but by candlelight
they will travel to places
implausibly silken,
each a virgin touch;
excited corpuscles collide
and just as our wrappings
change so completely
we are reminded
of what it means to be new.

Indecent

Curled in the tub,
he grasps at the Picasso
that lives in the chrome
until hot water fills the basin
formed by his legs and stomach;

heavy, the itch and burn
of grime prods his quivering
fingers to find and rip the wax
covering from the soap;

past pain, past blood,
the film fills in his nail marks
as he scrubs bar soap to splinters,
bubbles cling to his exterior,

but inside a gritty twinge
fleeces his bones where suds
cannot slake the sleaze
so concealed—

so impossible to reach.

Phantom Sensation

It is said that when a body is severed,
and defective limbs or organs are exorcised
from the whole, that their memories linger;

synapses that tied this piece to that
fire blanks out of habit, conjuring a pang or an itch
hovering in that approximate place in open air,

where once there was a toe, finger
elbow, knee, or even a lobe of lung
flexing, moving, filling.

As I write this, my phone buzzes against my thigh
and I dig in my pocket, finding only lint
in a pit of deflated denim

and I wonder at what point
this combination of plastic, glass,
and circuit boards became

so connected that some synapse fired,
from boredom or habit, calling
my hand to its absence.

Ephemeral Comprehension

Most would have called him old,
the man in the box, arms crossed over
a bundle of daffodils.
His silver mane was parted eternally left
Beneath his woolen hunting cap;
with networks of anger and laugh and love lines
carved deep, running together
from brow, to cheek, to chin;
he had seven children
who bore fifteen,
who then spawned nine more;

but he was young to Eleanor.
Slumped in a wheelchair,
her stoic features whispered *family*;
she lifted her gaze to her own progeny,
who gathered behind her, and she asked—
How old was he?

When she heard *Eighty two,*
she worked her jaw, blinked her eyes,
and as though it were guided
by some external force, she raised her arm
so slowly, so awkwardly to her chest,
and she breathed *younger than me.*

Her head swayed in an absent nod,
as though she felt the weight of being
the last of the first generation of this family
to settle across an ocean;
as though her mind had wafted back in time
to when all her brothers and sisters were young
rolling up the rug to polka on the bare boards
of the living room floor;
she knew then the inevitability
of what lurked before her.

But she did not know then that
she would wake the next morning with no memory
of the waxy complexion of her last sibling
to journey from this existence
to another existence,
or nonexistence,
or to all possible existences,
comingling in a glorious chaotic melancholy
of faith and faithlessness,
of hope and hopelessness,
in a plethora of oneness.

What she did know is that in that moment,
she simply was the sister
who had helped raise him from the coal bucket
the one who offered him a second chance at life,
hoping that for him it was one worth living.

Mind the Trolls

Bait the trolls carefully
for sometimes they bite back
so fiercely that they
conjure nightmares
worthy of Nocnitsa;

their long shadows pounce on you,
gripping you with their knees,
and with blades light as air
and black as obsidian,
they trace the trough
between your ribs;

should they bite,
you may need to call
on the witch rider
and she will come
to gather what plagues you,
placating them with simple boxes,
and she will hold your wounds
in the bower of her hand,
and bend her neck to clean them,

but it will be too late then
and not even circles of salt
or fistfuls of iron filings
flung in her face
will keep her
from knowing the taste of you;

she will have you then;
she will own you completely.

In the Shire

At the start
mud squelches between his bare toes
in the sodden labyrinth
of prairie grass and wild flowers,
as moonlit meditations lead him
to the screen house at the end of the trail;

there he sits silent;
the night breeze strums the strings
of the mesh shelter around him;
the trill in the trees
counters the bellied thrums
of bullfrogs in the water;
a black bear snuffle-grunts
in the brush beside him, hidden
in the shadows of the undergrowth;

when the wind shifts the bear leaves
and the man turns back
toward his rented cabin;
without light to steal the stars,
his walking stick sparks against the gravel,
mosquitoes feast
but he does not swat—

he knows that he is food
to the world that feeds him.

Commute

Counting down highway exits,
chin tipping to my chest,
I calculate the odds

that I left my body impaled
by a guardrail along the interstate,
thrown from the tangled Suzuki

we bought before the move from Georgia.
Blinking at Baldwin, my eyes open
on Lake Mallalieu, less than a mile

from the big house we bought
last winter, and I wonder what happened
to the last 20 miles of my trip home.

In the black of night
I click the garage door opener
without effect, and wonder

whether it is I or the batteries
that are most likely dead,
staring at the inches collecting

on the unshoveled drive, noticing
for the first time, the numbness
in the tips of my fingers.

The Wicker Woman

In pirouette,
against sepia skies
she sprouts, leg-over-leg,
cheese cloth webs
draped from her arms
like fine lace.

A German pointer
sniffs the tip of her long finger,
then moves to nuzzle the crowd
resolute beside her;
they thumb smartphones
shoulder-to-shoulder on the hill
as if to say to the wicker woman,

we are with you, waiting,
ready for the flames.

III.

Standoff on a Hair Trigger

When Alan Alda told a North Korean
"the war can't last forever,"
I stood on the 38th parallel, watching the
starlight reflect off the edge of the razor wire,
a concrete slab suspended,
between 50-year-old minefields
bedded in sands of scrutiny.

Pinned between eras, antique weapons posed
for tourists who thought the war long ended—
but like the Centralia coal seam,
embers of hostility smoldered beneath the surface
impossible to extinguish,
baking the soil
blessed by blood
daring us all to breathe.

Virginia Napalm

Oh, it got hot in '99
    when Corey and John
        cracked the cover of the
            Anarchist Cookbook

and found a recipe
    for *Virginia napalm*
        and *nerd bombs.*
            Their brew

curdled, popped, and snapped
    to a tacky goo.
        Corey stirred it
            in the red Hills Brother's

coffee can before
    they declared war
        on the old barn in Bedford,
            already crippled by dry rot;

they watched it
    smolder into flame
        while the windowpanes warped
            and burst—like buckeyes in

the iron belly of
    a woodstove.
        The glow crept up to
            tickle the old hay mound

tonguing at the asbestos shingles—
    and they watched, indifferent,
        as if nothing
            was more important.

The Carpet

Under ten years of deadfall
was soft earth, black as tar;
the wiry roots
of the new growth
crawled through
a roll of orange shag,
older than the house we lived in.

Saplings impaled the carpet,
tying each layer
to whatever it was
that lay at core of the thing,
that lured the roots
there to feed.

When the earth finally yielded,
a russet stain at the center of the mass
called to mind the image of blood,
and I wondered what blood would look like
if buried ten years on in the old woods
that would become my back yard.

The sodden fibers were heavy
as I heaved and I threaded it
between two trees along the fence line,
and up the hill to the gate,
until it wedged itself on the stump
of the old cherry tree that we burned
in the fire pit last spring.

Nothing else to do, I fetched
a blade and held it
willing the carpet empty
as I sawed at its thatched bottom;
inexplicably bright, clean threads
were shed as I cut, falling to the ground
like dandruff on a bedspread in winter.

I imagined the blade grinding on bone,
catching on the matted hair
or thick sweater of the corpse.
I practiced telling of my discovery
to the village police officers
who would call the Sheriff,
who would call the FBI,
who would call a family in need of closure;

I practiced my no comments for cameras
that would soon be camping on my lawn
and felt the anger sparked by the vulgarity
of the spectacle they'd bring down
upon this tiny riverside town,
and the rumors that would drive us out.

That is until my blade struck dirt,
and finding neither meat,
nor bone—human or otherwise—
I sighed, relieved, and lifted
each segment of carpet free
of the trees, and let them fall
into the steel dumpster
that waited in our drive.

      I turned, chancing one last glance
      at the stain there and told myself
      there was no blood. It had to be wine,
      that's all.

Recycler's Remorse

There was a time in my youth
when most things fed flame
in the barrel at the edge of our yard
and when the crumbled heap
of ash poured through the steel,
all of it was dumped in the brush
adjacent the end of an aging
leach bed where refined shit
seeped into the ground
where the swamp pressed
against the shade of the forest;

but that was before today's fees
and the laws requiring the use
of undersized recycle bins
brimful with cardboard packaging,
loose toilet paper tubes,
chipped root beer bottles,
and empty soup cans.
Each week, I roll the bin to the curb,
where it awaits the over-sized trucks
with matching logos,
and for that moment, I am alleviated
of this practice of collecting
boxes, glass, and aluminum,
and overfilling the red-lidded bin,
leaving half the recyclables
in my garage for next week,
despite the fact that the black-lidded trash bin
remains half-empty
and I fight the impulse to fill it
and rid us of all remaining refuse,

but I can't abide my conscience
when I think of the manmade mountains
spewing methane through flame-capped pipes,
knowing that they will fill too soon,
and it would likely be my soup cans
that would cause the space to run out.

Danforth House
(Savannah, GA)

Our guide shared stories
contented in her "facts"—
certain about the transcendent
truths of Savannah.
Just a working-class family
she chanted, presenting
the 18th Century Italian marble
fireplaces, detailed molding,
thousand-dollar colonial tea sets,
the *supplemental income* gained
from renting "his people" out
for petty cash spent on Madeira wine,
European fashions,
and a northern education;
when he dropped dead in 1827
his body lay in the parlor
before his life was catalogued
for posterity;
yellow fever did it, and I think
how befitting an end that was
for a southern gentleman of the day.
It was a different time she said.
Not the point, I thought—
he was still a hypocrite
founding a fortune
on the backs of slaves,
the faceless who remained
unnamed, unentitled
unhuman.

Spring Again

(at age 8)

Crows caw at the edge of the garden;
they peck and scratch at the fresh compost
where we piled it in winter;

they pick at the egg shells, rotten potatoes,
squash rinds, and bushels of apples turned
to mush and vinegar;

the snow melts and pools in our front yard;
it forms twin lakes, split by the driveway,
flooding everything

from where the willows budding whips
bless the sod, to the shallow ditch
that empties where the leach bed ends;

what's left of last season's cabbage
lies sweet in Brace's fields down
where the valley meets the ridgeline;

at the edge of Tamarack Swamp,
the Hackeranians thread dynamite
once more through the beaver dams;

the beavers know what's coming;
they migrate enmasse to the temporary pools
of our front yard, their bulbous bodies more massive

than they appear in picture books;
but when the blast is felt,
they return to their place out back,

gnawing the poplars and sugar maples
along the water's edge;
they always rebuild.

Everything in Its Place

Until C.J. Craig met with the Cartographers
for Social Equality, I had never considered
how my view of the world was skewed,
and everything I knew had been filtered
through a pane of 16th Century, European glass,

as if all truths were an approximation,
based on vague estimations
of my ancestors
obsessed with the size of their cod pieces
standing in history with their boots
on the throats of the other.
I had not heard of the Peters Projection,
nor had I questioned the size of Greenland
on the map from sixth-grade geography,
nor truly considered the top-down mentality
fostered by the orientation of random compass points.

After all, in the vacuum of space,
who is to say that north and south are not inversed
or that our four compass points do not form an hour glass
through which fictions fall,
until the sand strips the flesh
and your bleached bones lay naked
on the beaches of the Americas, Africa,
Australia, and Asia, realizing only then
how much we make of the trivial differences,
and how alike we truly are.

White Noise

Shots fired in Ferguson,
and blame is flung
like beads on an abacus
as police wrapped in riot gear
grip their assault weapons
against a city that burns.

Teargas is lobbed between people
as political pundits labor over statistics
of race and the implications
of stand-your-ground,
of the rights of lead
to be loosed.

Across the nation, protesters gather
outside clinics, promising all to the desperate—
clothes for children, money for rent.
They repel patients with propaganda,
only to slut shame them
when their babies burst from their bellies.

In the next election,
candidates claim
color-coded philosophies,
turning over cable news mantras
like marbles in their mouths—
we freedom, they slave,
we righteous, they devil,
we right, they wrong;

voters debate birth control,
validity of anthropomorphic corporations,
the right of steel to tear at living flesh,
debating which extremities could be mended
and at what cost to which insurance companies;
the moronic cluck at one another,
spinning a veil of white noise
to keep us separate, to misdirect our rage,
lulling us all to sleep.

Rain

Rain fell against the plastic shelter,
and the occupied cots shivered
to the rhythmic patter so like the gunfire
in the distance that sparked the exodus
from South Sudan.

New arrivals settled into the narrow
dirt aisles between the bunks
breathing;
thankful that at least there was air enough
here for them.

In the corner mothers whispered in Nuer
while newborns suckled and screamed
at dry breasts,
waiting
for the milk to come down.

When the thunder started,
an aid worker lifted a five-year old girl
from the shelter's entrance, her mother spoke
of polio—the only Nuer word
that needed no translation.

And still the rain fell
against the plastic,
the same as it would
against a tent in Minnesota,
and it fell in the same rhythm

as it would 7,000 miles away from
the frontlines of the world,
in a place where the sound
conjures only thoughts of Jiffy Pop
ballooning over a campfire.

> There other people are
> breathing and waiting,
> but for very different things.

Tears of Johannesburg

Clouds grieve over Johannesburg.
Their underbellies slit
by the needle top of Hillbrow Tower
until the streets surge.
In the alleys on higher ground,
good Samaritans pick their battles,
choosing which woman's screams to answer
and after how long.

In the pubs, voices chant
You can't save them all
while a government worker
speaks of the need for condoms
in a city where bruises bloom
on cheeks of wives
and sisters
and daughters
without any apparent cause
without any sign of ceasing.

In Cape Town,
there are just 100 days left in the dams,
fields crack between rows of signs
from Monsanto, DuPont, Syngenta.
At least there is food from last season,
graywater to flush the toilets,
and hope enough for the woman
clinging an infant to herself,
staring up at dispersed contrails
seeing them as potential clouds

> anything to bring
> the tears from Johannesburg
> to fill the rivers tomorrow.

Hitch

He sweeps back the skeletal remains
of his chemo-thin hair, and scratches
at the subsiding stubble on his chin;

leaning in over the podium,
he labors over the gravitas
of incarnate truth

cleaving to notions
of his own perishability, and we stare
at a man nearing his terminus;

even after his end, we linger
on what he skimmed
from the murky depths,

through thickets too dense to see,
over grounds too porous to stand on
discovering the dogma that acts upon us;

he speaks of compulsory love,
demanded by the *celestial dictatorship*
that bids us to love nothing more than it;

surrender your reason, and watch
an omnipotent game player, the great
deceiver, burn the only world

we know to exist—
and with it goes all
that is worth living for.

Beyond the Butterscotch

At age six, I had enough of the lint-covered
butterscotch hard candy passed to me
by the apathetic old man at the end of our pew;

during each Mass, my mother stood and filed down the aisle,
took the host on her tongue, and the old man slid me a stale,
sticky disc that absorbed bits of its own wrapper;

in catechism, we were forbidden to ask of the hypocrisy
of the teacher's pending annulment, or
of murder committed by soldiers overseas;

we thumbed rosary beads, memorized the creed
that told of a *begotten* Jesus, and defined the virgin
of one *holy catholic and apostolic church;*

without ever knowing of sex,
we were told to take it on faith
that parroting these words would spare us eternal torment,

saving us from sadistic stories of devil and demons
that torment all the children who behaved
only as designed, who could not resist their nature;

at six, the old man offered, and I took his candy,
but as the sugar subsided, I discovered embedded
grit that could not nourish and cellophane that could not save.

A telling reconciliation.

When a priest teases you in the confessional
about "losing your cherry,"
you come to understand that
it takes more than a Roman collar to gain enlightenment,
but then you wonder—

is he imagining you
downing the amoretto
till you are sprawled out
on the stained, sweat-soaked carpet;
is he visualizing her,
cleaving the clothes from your half-conscious body,
squeezing you between her thighs,
thinking of his own urges,
making these vague details of your drunken stupor
something tangible enough to warm him
in his bed chamber?

What would you do when he bit his lip,
and you were gripped by the desire to
open your vein in front of him—
the one you traced a thousand times as a child,
the one that would make it so easy
if you weren't so chicken?

The thought alone will cost you a Hail Mary,
and the action a rosary—maybe two—
but it is a small price, almost worth it,
to remind him that, human as we are,
it's best not to take matters of the soul so lightly.

Deserted City

The doors to LORD
are closed now;
the library,
where my aunt worked
was dismantled, shipped
south to another state,
its bones here reduced
to red-bricked rubble
tucked into piles
behind chain-link
and razor wire.

Across town
the mills rot in the sun
along the new Bayfront connection;
corroded sheet-metal eaves
crumble under their own weight
just visible over the stamped concrete walls.

The oily stink of new blacktop
hangs off State Street
where rusted-out,
over-priced cars
replaced the Koehler Brewery,
two-blocks away
from the site
of another bankruptcy auction
at Lovell Manufacturing.

Just outside the city proper,
GE Transportation restructured
for future economic growth,
abandoning the borough that it built
back at a time when barbers
still bled their patrons
in an effort to correct another imbalance
that never existed.

Daniel Ruefman's poetry and prose has appeared in more than 30 publications, including most recently in *Adelaide Magazine, Barely South Review, Burningword, Junto Magazine, Minetta Review, Red Earth Review, Sediments Literary-Arts Journal,* and the *Wisconsin Poets Calendar,* among others. He is the author of two collections of poetry, *Breathe Automatic* (2014) and *Sleep Bringer* (2019), both from Finishing Line Press. He is also an experienced editor, co-editing *Applied Pedagogies: Strategies for Online Writing Instruction* (Utah State University Press, 2016), and *The HitchLit Review.*

Daniel holds several degrees in writing, including a BA from Edinboro University, MA from Slippery Rock University, and a Ph.D. from Indiana University of Pennsylvania. A native of Pennsylvania, he currently lives in Wisconsin where he works as an Associate Professor of Rhetoric and Composition at the University of Wisconsin—Stout.

www.ingramcontent.com/pod-product-compliance
Lightning Source LLC
Chambersburg PA
CBHW021203090426
42740CB00008B/1209